THEN   NOW

RIVERSIDE

OPPOSITE: An 1877 depiction of Riverside from Mount Rubidoux shows a town founded seven years earlier by two abolitionists, Judge John W. North and Dr. James P. Greves, of the Southern California Colony Association. An early visit to the town site provided the following impression: "A bare, dry, sun-kissed and wind-swept mesa stretched for miles to the south." (Courtesy Riverside Metropolitan Museum.)

THEN NOW

RIVERSIDE

Glenn Edward Freeman

Bird's Eye View of **RIVER SIDE**, San Bernardino Co., Cal.

LOOKING NORTH TO THE SAN BERNARDINO MOUNTAINS.

This book is dedicated to my late mother and father,
Virginia Louise and Charles Edward Freeman.

Copyright © 2009 by Glenn Edward Freeman
ISBN 978-0-7385-7079-2

Library of Congress Control Number: 2009924703

Published by Arcadia Publishing
Charleston, South Carolina

Printed in the United States of America

Then and Now is a registered trademark and is used under license from
Salamander Books Limited

For all general information contact Arcadia Publishing at:
Telephone 843-853-2070
Fax 843-853-0044
E-mail sales@arcadiapublishing.com
For customer service and orders:
Toll-Free 1-888-313-2665

Visit us on the Internet at www.arcadiapublishing.com

ON THE FRONT COVER: Looking east from Mount Rubidoux is a *c.* 1900 view of downtown Riverside with Main Street at center. Clearly visible on the left is Eighth Street, now University Avenue. On the right is Tenth Street. Noticeably absent is the 1903 Riverside County Courthouse. Most of the taller buildings in downtown Riverside were built after the 1960s. (Then image courtesy Riverside Metropolitan Museum; now image courtesy author.)

ON THE BACK COVER: In this 1889 photograph taken looking north on Main Street near Tenth Street is what would become Riverside City Hall. On the far right is the Rowell–later Reynolds–Hotel, with towers from both the Castleman, in the center of the right side, and YMCA buildings visible. In the distance, on the left, is the nearly completed tower for the 1890 Loring Building. (Courtesy Riverside Metropolitan Museum.)

CONTENTS

ACKNOWLEDGMENTS

I would like to thank local historian Steve Lech for allowing access to his extensive postcard collection as well as providing historical information and suggestions. This book is also greatly indebted to Kevin Hallaran and the Riverside Metropolitan Museum, without which the majority of the fine historical photographs would not have been possible.

Several individuals, to whom I am very thankful, helped in assembling the book: Georgia Gordon Sercl, Velda and Norman Kelly, Daniel Balboa, Scott Taylor, Helen Richardson and Rich McCarthy, JoAnne Pease-Simpson, George Porter, Lorrie Walker and Steve Faure, Judy Avery, Corol Cree, Dan Bernstein, Robert Quezada, John Gettis, Pat Delahunty, and Judy Whitson. In particular, Kimberly Pierceall was very helpful during the crafting and reviewing of the text. I would also like to thank Gina, Cindy, Pam, and Suzanne for their support.

Likewise, several institutions provided important resources, including Tony Zbaraschuk of La Sierra University, Sean Faustina of Riverside Plaza, Laurel Dickerson of Stater Brothers Markets, Brett Perry and Jim Hall at HistoricAerials.com, Michelle Sifuentes at March Field Air Museum, and Bruce Ward of Riverside International Automotive Museum. Also, Jessica Herdina, Ruth McCormick, and Cathy Nguyen of the Riverside Public Library's Local History Resource Center were of great assistance during the research portion of the project. In particular, the library's local subject files were most valuable.

This entire process could not have been possible without Arcadia Publishing. I would like to thank Debbie Seracini, Devon Weston, and Scott Davis, all of whom made the process as simple as possible.

Finally, I would be remiss without thanking local historians, and in particular the late Tom Patterson of the *Press-Enterprise*, whose local history books and newspaper columns proved both inspirational and invaluable during the research process. Also, the many local history books of Joan H. Hall were very useful. I hope this book helps inspire future generations to continue documenting Riverside's history.

Except where indicated, all "then" photographs are courtesy of the Riverside Metropolitan Museum. Unless indicated, all "now" photographs were taken by the author in late 2008 and early 2009. Thanks to Thomas D. Lamm for assisting with some "now" photographs.

INTRODUCTION

From humble beginnings in 1870 to postwar expansion and explosive suburban growth, which continues to this day, Riverside transformed from a citrus pioneer into the largest city within a region of four million residents. As one of California's oldest municipalities, the city's early success in citrus spawned the growth that made Riverside the seat of county government and home to civic, cultural, and educational institutions not found in nearby cities.

But as with all cities, and Southern California as a whole, Riverside changed throughout the years. Some might say for the better, some might say otherwise. In reality, the truth likely rests somewhere in between, no doubt colored as much by our age as by our experiences. And now, with the help of Arcadia Publishing, the opportunity to explore this change in an easy-to-digest "then & now" photographic format is possible.

Whether viewing an iconic street scene from a hundred years ago or comparing today's Riverside Plaza with the original, each set of photographs showcases what has changed—or, in some cases, has not changed. For longtime residents, the photographs offer the chance to relive a few of those long cherished sights from yesteryear, while for recent arrivals, or those much younger in age, they provide the opportunity to see what once existed.

By comparing and contrasting photographs taken from the same vantage point several decades apart, this book provides a glimpse into how Riverside began and how the town developed. It is my hope this unique format will both teach and inspire others to begin exploring not only the city's past but the future as well.

CHAPTER 1

DOWNTOWN

Built five years after the city's founding, the B. D. Burt and Brothers general merchandise store was Riverside's first brick building in 1875. Modified throughout the decades, the building (above, around 1880) stood at the northwest corner of Eighth Street, now University Avenue, and Main Street for nearly 100 years before being replaced with a bank's 11-story office building in 1973.

Probably no other entity has had a greater impact on Riverside than the Mission Inn. Seen below around 1885 from Main Street, the Glenwood Hotel, built in 1876 as a 12-room family home and guest house, was replaced by a much larger and more luxurious mission-style hotel in 1903.

By 1931, after several expansions, the Mission Inn encompassed an entire city block, helping to inspire Mission Revival architecture throughout Southern California. (Then image courtesy Riverside Local History Center.)

An 1886 view of dirt-covered Main Street, as seen looking south from the area around Sixth Street, resembles an old western film rather than Riverside 100 years later, with a quarter-million residents. In the center is the new Castleman Building, home to Riverside First National Bank. The early 2009 photograph is prior to an extensive refurbishment of the Main Street Pedestrian Mall, which replaced four blocks of Main Street in 1966.

A west view down Eighth Street, now University Avenue, toward Main Street shows bicycle riders and horse carriages traversing the unpaved road around 1895. In the center are the Castleman (left) and Evans (right) buildings. In early 2009, the same view from the intersection of Lemon Street shows taller palm trees and buildings, including the 11-story California Tower, which opened in 1973 as Security Pacific National Bank.

By 1900, several businesses lined the streets of downtown, including Eighth Street, as seen below from the northwest corner of Orange Street. On the left are the *Daily Enterprise* and William Peter's Carriage and Buggy Shop. On the far right is the Castleman Building. Today the street is completely transformed. From left to right, it includes the 1928 Arcade Building, the 1904 Roosevelt Building, and the four-story 1911 Riverside First National Bank.

Looking east down Eighth Street from Main Street in 1905 below are the Evans (left) and Castleman (right) Buildings, two of Riverside's most ornate structures. In 1911, Riverside First National Bank replaced the Castleman with a larger, four-story building (above, right). Housing two of Riverside's largest banks, the intersection would remain the city's primary financial district for several decades.

Located at the northeast corner of Eighth and Main Streets, the Evans Building is Riverside's most significant historic building to have been demolished, according to many. Built by civic leader S. C. Evans in 1891 to house his Riverside National Bank, the building's ornate cupola was removed around 1907. A wrecking ball brought down the rest of the building in 1964, although the lot has remained empty since that time. Note the semicircular pattern of bricks (below, left) still visible atop the nearby building.

Located at the southeast corner of Eighth and Main Streets, the Castleman Building, above, was constructed in 1886 for Riverside First National Bank. The building below, designed by Parkinson Architects of Los Angeles, replaced the Victorian-style Castleman in 1911. Following a merger in 1915, Citizens National Bank and Trust moved in. By the 1960s, the bank was the inland headquarters for the Los Angeles–based Security Pacific National Bank. In 2006, University of California Riverside's Sweeney Art Gallery opened on the ground floor.

In 1930, the S. H. Kress dime store, below, opened on the east side of Main Street between Eighth and Ninth Streets. At various times, nearby competitors included Sears, Montgomery Ward, J.C. Penney, Woolworth's, and Pic 'N Save. When it closed in late 1980, it was one of the last Kress stores remaining and the last of the downtown chains. In April 1990, the University of California Riverside–California Museum of Photography opened. According to the museum, it contains one of the largest photograph and camera collections in the nation.

Below is a view of Main Street looking north toward Eighth Street from near Ninth Street around 1940. On the right are the Rouse, Kress, Citizen's Bank, and Evans (sans cupola) buildings with the Mission Inn in the distance. Though nearly all the buildings at right remain in 2009, large trees along the Main Street Pedestrian Mall obscure the view. (Then image courtesy author.)

R-65—Main Street, Riverside, California

The photograph above, taken around 1960 of the west side of Main Street from Ninth Street, shows downtown's main retail area prior to the proliferation of suburban shopping. The dark-colored building is Keystone Drugs on Main Street at University Avenue, one of several drugstores once located on Main Street. At the center of the photograph are the towers of the Hayt and Loring Buildings, situated at the corner of Main Street and Seventh Street, now Mission Inn Avenue. The same view in 2009 shows modern buildings on the left. (Then image courtesy Steve Lech.)

This 1950s view of Main Street looking north from Eighth Street, now University Avenue, shows the distinctive towers for the Hayt and Loring Buildings (left). The towers sat opposite one another for several decades until the early 1970s, when the west side of Main Street between University Avenue and Seventh Street, now Mission Inn Avenue, was razed for the 11-story Security Pacific National Bank plaza. The same view in early 2009 (below) shows refurbishment of the 1966 Main Street Pedestrian Mall underway. (Then image courtesy Steve Lech.)

Looking north on Main Street at its intersection with Tenth Street, the one-year-old Main Street Pedestrian Mall is pictured below in 1967. On the right is the 1903 Pennsylvania Building, which once housed the headquarters for local grocer A. M. Lewis. The 1975 opening of city hall (above) spanning Main Street provided a southern anchor for the four-block mall. In late 2008, the first phase of mall refurbishment was completed. (Then image courtesy author.)

In 1886, the Riverside Banking Company—headed by Otis T. Dyer—opened on the northwest corner of Main Street at Ninth Street, below. Other businesses included SeBrell and Cover Druggists and Patton and McLeod Hardware. In 1938, a new structure was built to house Bank of America, which moved from the nearby Loring Building. In 1976, Bank of America relocated to Fourteenth Street. In 1984, a parking structure (above) for the adjacent Mission Square office building was built on the corner.

The International Order of Odd Fellows building (above, around 1910) opened as Public Hall in 1878. Over the ensuing decades, the building at the southwest corner of Main Street and Ninth Street served as home to several fraternal organizations, including both the Masons and Odd Fellows. In 1969, the building was razed for city hall, which was completed in 1975. In 2008, Ninth Street (below) was reopened after being closed since the 1966 construction of the pedestrian mall.

Located at the southeast corner of Main Street and Ninth Street, the 1887 Rowell Hotel (above, around 1900) is best known as the Reynolds Hotel following the 1902 purchase by George N. Reynolds, who operated a department store directly across Ninth Street. In 1940, F. W. Woolworth opened on the site and remained there until 1957, when the store moved to the Riverside Plaza. By 1975, the site became part of city hall.

The Central Block, in the photograph below around 1940, opened in the early 1890s as the Oppenheimer Building. Located on the west side of Main Street between Eighth Street and Ninth Street, the building's exterior featured Victorian bay windows. The last owner, Arthur B. White, purchased the building in 1906, with an office there until his death in 1975 at the age of 99. By 1984, the six-story Mission Square office project (above) replaced all other businesses on the entire block.

Originally opened in 1900, Franzen Hardware became Westbrook's following a 1935 fire. In 1959, the store was sold to Imperial Hardware, which in 1964 renamed the store and erected a modern false front over the art deco facade. Although Imperial Hardware moved to the Tyler Mall in 1972, the false-front design remained until June 2007. (Then image courtesy Helen Richardson and Rich McCarthy.)

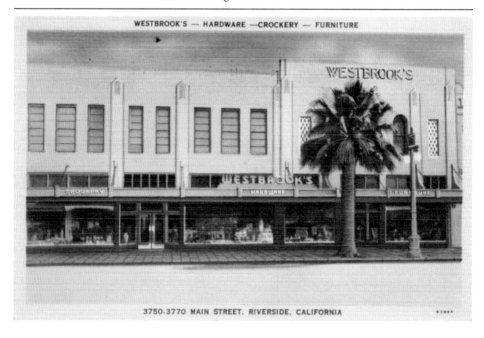

WESTBROOK'S — HARDWARE —CROCKERY — FURNITURE

WESTBROOK'S

3750-3770 MAIN STREET, RIVERSIDE, CALIFORNIA

The Rubidoux Building (above, 1920s) was one of Riverside's larger brick buildings originating in the late 1800s. Located at the southeast corner of Main Street and Seventh Street, the building once included Banks Drug Company. In 1938, a relocated Sears moved into the art deco structure (below) that replaced the original building. Sears remained there until its much larger, suburban-style store opened on Arlington Avenue in 1964. After Sears, the building housed antique stores, including Mission Galleria.

Located at the southwest corner of Main Street and Sixth Street, the three-story Frost Building (above, 1930s) was built in 1892 by George Frost. In 1921, this building became one of four different downtown locations for the Ark Housefurnishing store. In 1940, now known as the Backstrand Building, it was completely renovated. The modernization included removal of the top floor, which once housed a local National Guard unit.

The southeast corner of Eighth and Lemon Streets has a long history with furniture stores, including the Ark (below, around 1900), Huffman's, and McMahan's. A 1924 fire at the Motor Transit Company destroyed the building. The Aurea Vista Hotel (above) replaced the structure in 1927. Designed by local architect G. Stanley Wilson, the Spanish-Moorish building included 20 guest rooms and a stately ballroom with a balcony.

The Arlington Hotel, below, located at the northwest corner of Eighth Street and Lime Street, served as the county's first offices. Built in 1887 by H. B. Everest, the hotel was purchased by Frank A. Tetley in 1912. The hotel was renamed Tetley Hotel by Tetley's daughter in 1958. In 1972, a fire destroyed the then-named Riverside Hotel. The long vacant lot (above) is primed to become the new location of Fire Station No. 1.

The Hotel Holyrood (above, around 1900), located at the southwest corner of Market Street and Eighth Street, is one of the oldest commercial structures remaining in downtown. Built in 1884, the exterior was modernized in 1924 by the new owner, Pliny T. Evans, who renamed the building Hotel Plaza. In 1980, a 10-story building was proposed for the location, but recently, the site was selected as the future location for the Riverside School for the Arts.

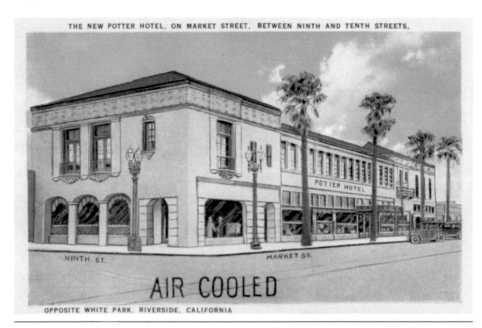

THE NEW POTTER HOTEL, ON MARKET STREET, BETWEEN NINTH AND TENTH STREETS.

NINTH ST.   MARKET ST.

AIR COOLED

OPPOSITE WHITE PARK, RIVERSIDE, CALIFORNIA

Built in the mid-1920s by Sidney E. Potter of Stahlman and Potter Construction Company, the Potter Hotel (above, around 1927) was located on the southeast corner of Market and Ninth Streets. In 1926, the building housed the Citrus Belt Building and Loan Association. By 1967, the building's southern half had been removed. It has since been renamed the White Park Building and has housed Riverside Mission Florist for several years. (Then image courtesy Helen Richardson and Rich McCarthy.)

Riverside High School, seen below from the southwest corner of Ninth and Lime Streets shortly after opening in 1902, served both boys and girls separately before becoming an administrative office in 1924. The building was sold to the city in 1949 and demolished shortly thereafter. Although a federal building was once proposed for the block, instead, the site was used for parking until the $20-million Riverside Centre office complex (above) opened in 1982. Initially, its primary tenant was IBM, which relocated from 3610 Fourteenth Street.

Located at the northeast corner of Fourteenth and Brockton Streets, the three-story brick building seen below served both elementary and high school students when it opened in 1889. The name changed to Grant School in 1901 upon the relocation of the high school to a new building at Ninth and Lemon Streets. Following the 1933 Long Beach earthquake, the Gothic-influenced building was razed and replaced with today's Spanish-style Grant Elementary School, which became the Grant Education Center in 2008.

Designed by Los Angeles architect Franklin Pierce Burnham, the 1903 Riverside County Courthouse is considered one of the finest examples of Beaux Arts architecture in the nation. The courthouse, patterned after the Grand Palais and Petite Palais from the 1900 Paris Exposition, received a G. Stanley Wilson–designed Orange Street addition in 1930. A 1950s proposal to expand onto the front lawn was rejected due to community opposition. In 1995, the courthouse underwent a three-year, $25-million restoration and seismic upgrade.

Womens Club Building,
Riverside, Cal.

Built in 1908, the Riverside Women's Club (above, around 1910) and Masonic temple (left) were located at the southeast corner of Eleventh and Main Streets. After relocating to Tenth and Brockton Streets in 1915, the women's club sold the building to the Elks lodge, which remained until 1956. By the mid-1960s, a new retail building replaced the classical structure. Since 1991, the site has been occupied by the Robert Presley Hall of Justice. (Then image courtesy Helen Richardson and Rich McCarthy.)

Seen below in the 1920s, the 1892 Fredericks Building was located on the west side of Main Street between Sixth and Seventh Streets. The building, once owned by the widow of writer Robert Louis Stevenson, was the home to the popular Mapes Cafeteria from 1920 to 1956. In 1963, the building was torn down. The lot remained empty until a new structure housing the Tamale Factory restaurant was built in 2006. (Then image courtesy Steve Lech.)

Built in 1890, the Loring Building remains one of downtown's most ornate structures still standing from the late 1800s. Located at the northwest corner of Main Street and Mission Inn Avenue, the Romanesque building was remodeled in 1918, covering most of the gingerbread brick in stucco to match the adjacent Mission Inn. The building once housed Bank of America (below, around 1930) and later Diamond Lil nightclub. Since 1994, Citizens Business Bank has occupied the ground floor.

On the Seventh Street side of the Loring Building, the 900-seat Loring Opera House was Riverside's elegant showplace for both national and local productions. In 1920, the renamed Loring Theater (above, around 1927) began a slow conversion to motion pictures. By the time the theater closed in 1973, it was known as the Golden State Theater and showed second-run movies. The theater portion remained vacant for several years until succumbing to fire in October 1990.

Known as the Stalder Building, the structure located at the northeast corner of Market Street and Mission Inn Avenue, below, was originally built as three separate buildings, above, around 1900. In 1926, architect G. Stanley Wilson unified the buildings with a new Mission-style facade. Over the years, the structures have housed Fire Station No. 1, Glenwood Stables, Glenwood Garage, and several antique stores and eateries, including Mr. Beasley's Antiques and Vivian's Café.

Seen below around 1933 is the Market Street side of the Stalder Building. Originally built in 1904 for the Glenwood Garage, the building was later purchased by Gordon Stalder, who applied the new Mission-style architecture. For several years, the building housed Glenwood Motors, which sold and serviced Chryslers, Plymouths, and Willyses. The white building at left is Riverside Welding and Brazing Works. In 2008, the building was vacated to make way for the proposed Fox Plaza commercial and residential project.

The Riverside Fox Theater, seen below shortly after opening in 1929 as West Coast Riverside, was a favorite location for Hollywood sneak previews, according to newspaper reports, with the most celebrated being *Gone with the Wind* in 1939. Although successful for several decades, the theater fell on hard times following the advent of multiplex theaters. After years in limbo, work began in late 2007 on a $25-million renovation transforming the Hispanic Revival–style theater into a 1,600-seat performing arts venue.

2621 — FIRST METHODIST CHURCH RIVERSIDE, CALIFORNIA.

Located at the northeast corner of Sixth and Orange Streets, the First United Methodist Church of Riverside spawned four local Methodist churches—Arlington, Grace, Wesley, and Rubidoux. In 1902, a new building (above, around 1912) was built adjacent to the church's original 1876 brick chapel. After a devastating fire in 1947, the church moved to 4845 Brockton Avenue. The site has served Pacific Telephone and AT&T since the early 1950s. (Then image courtesy Steve Lech.)

2619 — BAPTIST CHURCH, RIVERSIDE, CALIFORNIA.

Originally built in 1880 and relocated to the northeast corner of Ninth and Lemon Streets in 1904, the First Baptist Church was the third church formed in Riverside. In 1908, the wooden building was completely refaced in brick, and it was expanded in 1928. After the congregation's 1965 move to 5500 Alessandro Boulevard, in 1982 the old downtown church was destroyed by fire. In 1987, the five-story J. F. Davidson office building opened. (Then image courtesy Steve Lech.)

Designed by Franklin Pierce Burnham of Los Angeles–based Burnham and Bleisner, downtown's Carnegie Library (below, around 1905) opened in 1903 as the city's first dedicated library building. It was expanded in the 1920s and assisted in the training for the acclaimed Riverside Library School for several years. In 1987, the Chinese Memorial Pavilion (above) was built near the location of the former Carnegie. Many say the 1965 demolition of the old library bolstered the historic preservation movement in Riverside.

Although younger generations have found favor in its striking, modern design, the Central Library, seen below in 1965, has suffered from harsh criticism since replacing the 1903 Carnegie Library. Designed by Riverside architect Bolton C. Moise Jr., the building, with its interwoven dove screens, is an excellent example of the mid-century New Formalism architecture popular during its construction. In early 2009, plans to raze the building for a larger library surfaced. (Then image courtesy Steve Lech.)

In 1945, Harold Taylor Sr. opened Taylor's Appliances at 4043 Main Street, where the store remained, across from the Riverside County Courthouse, until a 1972 fire destroyed the building. In 1973, Taylor's Appliances moved to Jurupa and Magnolia Avenues before relocating again in 1991 to 6140 Magnolia Avenue. In 1981, the false-front facade of a hotel was built at the former Main Street location and used during filming of the Walter Matthau and Jack Lemmon movie *Buddy Buddy*. (Then image courtesy Scott Taylor.)

Typical of many art deco grocery stores of its time, architect E. A. Thompson incorporated elements of "streamline moderne" into the 1936 Safeway store located at 4093 Market Street. Two competitors—Alpha Beta and Sage's—would soon sprout nearby. In 1961, the store became Miller's Surplus, forerunner to the Ontario-based Miller's Outpost—now Anchor Blue. The building received an extensive makeover in 2004.

Located at the southeast corner of Magnolia Avenue and Fourteenth Street, the Magnolia Drive-In Market (below, around 1931) was a collection of individual proprietors. Out of view at left is Newman Park, where a WPA-commissioned Juan Bautista de Anza statue was constructed in 1942.

A turn lane from northbound Magnolia Avenue to eastbound Fourteenth Street, which separated the site from the park, was removed in 1996, allowing for an expanded medical clinic, which had long-since replaced the original buildings.

A view south on Market Street from Seventh Street, below, shows the original Greyhound bus station around 1960. In the distance is the Potter Hotel building. Within a few years, the bus station would relocate across Market Street, and by 1975, the old bus site would become a parking garage (above, left) for the Security Pacific National Bank building, which opened two years earlier. The six-story Mission Square office building (above, center) opened in 1984. (Then image courtesy Steve Lech.)

Riverside, California

Built in the mid-1960s, the Greyhound bus station (above, around 1970) replaced the previous station located across the street at 3734 Market Street. Greyhound moved again to a consolidated bus facility that opened one block west in 1983. In the mid-1980s, plans for a 15-story office building surfaced for the Market Street property. However, the project was scaled back, and in 1990, the seven-story Riverside Metro Center and adjacent parking garage (below) opened. (Then image courtesy Steve Lech.)

In 1961, as part of a plan to bolster downtown shopping in the wake of suburban exodus, twin garages were built one block apart on the west side of Orange Street between Seventh and Ninth Streets. Used primarily for businesses along Main Street, the garages were downtown's response to the ease of parking found at newly built shopping centers, including the Riverside Plaza. In 2008 and 2009, the Googie-style garages received a new look (below).

In 1905, Fire Station No. 1 relocated from the present-day Stalder Building to Eighth Street near the northeast corner of Lime Street. It remained the main downtown fire station until a new building designed by Bolton C. Moise Jr. opened on Seventh Street at Lime Street in 1957. After the 1963 demolition of the station below, the site became a parking lot. In 1985, Winchell's Donut House—later Pizza Hut—opened on the adjacent lot. (Then image courtesy Daniel Balboa.)

Fred Stebler moved his blacksmith shop to Ninth and Vine Streets in 1909, eventually expanding into a larger brick building, below. In 1921, Stebler merged with competitor George Parker. The merged company would eventually become part of the Food Machinery Corporation, or F.M.C. By the 1960s, the building housed a bakery for Sage's Markets. In 2002, the newly refurbished Ironworks building, above, reopened as professional offices.

In 1904, the San Pedro, Los Angeles, and Salt Lake Railroad—later Union Pacific—opened a station on Vine Street south of Seventh Street. The exterior of the Mission Revival building was later modified, including the enclosure of the north patio, which has since been reopened. Passenger service was discontinued in 1971, and in 1977, the station was placed on the National Register of Historic Places. A fire heavily damaged the structure in 1982. Since 2000, it has been home to Coffee Depot.

In 1915, fairgoers across the region began flocking to Riverside for the Southern California Fair. The grandstands (above, 1926) were located along Market Street north of Fairmount Park. Though the annual fair ceased in 1930, semi-regular events continued into the 1950s. A fire destroyed the grandstands, and Highway 60 eventually bisected the former fairgrounds. Since 1980, the site slowly developed into a business park.

After occupying rented quarters at Ninth and Orange Streets, Riverside's Chinese residents relocated to a one-block street at the northwest corner of Brockton and Tequesquite Avenues in 1885 (below, around 1900). An 1893 fire wiped out many original structures; however, the town remained inhabited for several years. The last business closed in 1938. Its remaining resident, George Wong, stayed until his death in 1974. After sitting vacant for several decades, a medical office has been proposed recently for the site.

Seen below around 1887, the John T. Jarvis house, located on Twelfth Street near the base of Mount Rubidoux, is one of Riverside's most impressive early homes. Finished in 1888 at a cost of about $10,000, the Victorian-Gothic home was designed by A. W. Boggs. A 1914 alteration removed the tower and four dormer windows and added bungalow-style exterior elements, including a new front porch (above). The 11-room, three-story home remained in the Jarvis family until 1974.

A view northwest from Pachappa Hill around 1905 shows Mount Rubidoux without the Serra Cross, which was erected in 1907. Heading west from lower right to top left is Bandini Avenue. Within a few years, this area developed into the Wood Streets neighborhood. Below, in the distance, can be seen Mount Baldy (center) and the Cajon Pass (right).

Prior to the 1913 completion of the Magnolia fill project, which connected downtown to the newly extended Magnolia Avenue, the area between Jurupa Avenue and downtown was sparsely populated. Subdividing began soon thereafter on what became Riverside's very popular Wood Streets neighborhood. The name originated from the first subdivision—Homewood Court—by Dr. Edward H. Wood. By 1960, most of the subdividing was completed. (Then image courtesy Riverside Local History Center.)

CHAPTER

AROUND TOWN

Built in 1902 alongside Magnolia Avenue in the Arlington area, the Sherman Institute officially opened in 1903 after relocating from Perris. With the exception of the current Sherman Museum, the original buildings were demolished in 1969 and replaced with modern facilities. Now known as Sherman Indian High School, the campus serves as an off-reservation boarding school for Native Americans.

In 1920, Neighbors of Woodcraft, a fraternal benefit association for retirees, bought 45 acres of Magnolia Avenue near Adams Street to establish a retirement home. Local architect Henry L. A. Jekel designed the first buildings (below). The facility expanded to 75 acres before closing in 1952. In 1955, California Baptist College—now University—moved in. In 1965, a 113-acre enclosed shopping center, Magnolia Mall, was proposed but never built on the site. Recently, the campus has constructed several new buildings, including the Yeager Center (above, right).

In 1907, the University of California established the Citrus Experiment Station at the base of Mount Rubidoux. In 1918, a new station opened at the base of Box Springs Mountain (above), expanding its world-renown citrus research, which continues to this day. In 1954, academic studies were added, and in 1959, the school became a general University of California campus. By 2009, University of California Riverside boasted nearly 20,000 students, with the former citrus station housing the A. Gary Anderson Graduate School of Management.

Surrounded by barbed wire in the 1890s are the two original Washington navel orange trees from which all Southern California navels were derived. In 1902, both trees were replanted elsewhere; one still bears fruit today in a tiny park located at Magnolia and Arlington Avenues. The original Central Avenue homestead has long since been replaced with houses. However, a historic marker dedicated in 1935 identifies the location of the original 1875 plantings.

Porter's Courtesy Corner (below, around 1928) was opened in 1926 by brothers Frank and George Porter. Also seen is Smith's Market, which over the years would also house Pendred's Market, Waldo's Market, Magnolia West Liquors, and various mini-marts until 2000, when it became Flower Club. In the late 1950s, Century Barbers (above, center) opened, and it remains in business. The site is still owned and operated by Porter family descendants. (Then image courtesy George Porter.)

Below is a view east of Arlington Avenue at the intersection with Riverside Avenue around 1901. In 1957, the Riverside Freeway—Highway 91—opened through much of Riverside, causing the rerouting of Riverside Avenue where it connects with Arlington. In 1959, the Tavaglione family opened Tava Lanes on a portion of the site just east of the freeway. The bowling alley remained in operation until 2005 and was torn down in 2007.

Planning for Victoria Avenue, above around 1891 as viewed from Washington Street, began in the late 1880s as part of Matthew Gage's Arlington Heights subdivision. Named in honor of Britain's Queen Victoria, the 10-mile roadway was designed as a botanical garden by landscape architect Franz Hosp. A provision required adjacent property owners to plant and maintain street trees. In 2000, the divided parkway was added to the National Register of Historic Places. It remains one of the most unique drives within Southern California.

Founded in 1907, Grace United Methodist Church began at the intersection of Eighth and High, now Victoria, Streets. In 1956, the church moved to 1085 Linden Street near University of California Riverside. By 1963, the Thunderbird Lodge motel replaced the original church. In 2005, the lodge, which originally sported 1960s atomic-era architecture, underwent a complete makeover; however, the vintage neon sign remained. (Then image courtesy Grace United Methodist Church.)

Opened in April 1949 and seen below around 1950, Stater Brothers at 2933 Eighth Street was the second of three Stater Brothers grocery stores to open in the area during the late 1940s. The 10,000-square-foot store closed in June 1975. Later the building was occupied by a waterbed store and several grocery stores, including Sav-U-Foods in 1993 and El Pueblo Market in 1997. (Then image courtesy Stater Brothers Markets.)

Located at 6086 Magnolia Avenue, this Stater Brothers grocery store originally opened in September 1949. Seen below around 1968, looking toward Magnolia Avenue from Elizabeth Street, the original building was valued at $70,000. Stater Brothers closed the store in July 1980, at which time a Goodwill store (above) moved into the building. (Then image courtesy Stater Brothers Markets.)

Located on Magnolia Avenue across from Palm School—now Riverside Adult School—Fire Station No. 3 was built in the mid-1920s. The station's original address was 2640 but later became 6750 following street renumbering designed to reconcile the city's divergent but merging street grids. By the early 1960s, the station had been removed to make way for parking at the Brockton Arcade. Fire Station No. 3 is now located at 6395 Riverside Avenue. (Then image courtesy Daniel Balboa.)

Sage's Markets was a small, San Bernardino–based grocery chain with three Riverside locations before bankruptcy shuttered the chain in 1973. The 6491 Magnolia Avenue store (above, around 1965) originally started in 1947 as an A. M. Lewis grocery but was quickly sold to Sage's, which opened around 1949. In 1976, Thrifty Drug and Big 5 Sporting Goods moved in. Alin Party Supply and Victorian Salon and Day Spa later replaced Thrifty Drug. (Then image courtesy Steve Lech.)

Opened in three stages between 1956 and 1957, the original Riverside Plaza was one of Southern California's first major mall-like developments. The plaza (below, around 1960) included a Mayfair Market, an F. W. Woolworth, and a 204,000-square-foot Harris' department store, the first major suburban store for the San Bernardino–based retailer. In 1998, Fresno-based Gottschalks acquired the Harris' chain. In early 2009, Gottschalks filed for bankruptcy, and the building was sold to Los Angeles–based clothing retailer Forever 21. (Then image courtesy Steve Lech.)

Developed by Riverside's Heers Associates, the original open-air Riverside Plaza (below, around 1960) was designed by Art Jacobsen of Victor Gruen Associates. When the three-story—plus basement—Harris' department store opened in 1957, it contained the city's first escalators. At left is Woolworth's, and on the right is a Thom McAn shoe store. In 1984, the main corridor, seen above in 2009, received a roof, as the plaza became an enclosed mall during an extensive makeover. (Then image courtesy Steve Lech.)

This view of the Riverside Plaza around 1970 shows its second major anchor, W. T. Grants, which opened in 1966 and closed in 1975. At the far end beyond Grants is the original Vons grocery, which opened in 1967 and now faces Riverside Avenue. In 1976, Montgomery Ward moved into Grants. Montgomery Ward closed in 2001, and the plaza was remade back into an open-air center in 2004. (Then image courtesy Daniel Balboa.)

Built by Ernest W. Hahn, the $45-million Tyler Mall opened on October 12, 1970. The single-story mall contained 66 stores—eventually 85—with the Broadway and J.C. Penney department stores. After a three-year design delay, May Company opened at the south end in 1973. Following moderate makeovers in the 1970s and 1980s, a $100-million expansion in 1991 added a second level of shops, a fourth department store—Nordstrom—multi-level parking structures, and new name—Galleria at Tyler. (Then image courtesy Daniel Balboa.)

Originally opened with the Tyler Mall in 1970, the twin-theater United Artists Cinema, below, quickly expanded to four theaters. It remained Riverside's primary indoor multiplex for several years and was one of few inland-area theaters to show midnight movies—*Rocky Horror Picture Show, The Wall*—during the 1970s and 1980s. In 2001, the building was replaced with a Barnes and Noble bookstore (above). In 2008, a relocated T.G.I. Friday's restaurant adjoined the west (left) side of the building. (Then image courtesy Daniel Balboa.)

A view of the corner of Magnolia Avenue and Hughes Alley around 1966 shows George and Marie Leibert's home, below, prior to the construction of Farrell's Ice Cream Parlour, which opened with the Tyler Mall in 1970. Farrell's closed in the 1980s, and the building was later removed for parking. In 2007, the corner was redeveloped into the Galleria at Tyler's North Village, above, which included an AMC 16 theater complex and Yard House restaurant. (Then image courtesy Georgia Gordon Sercl.)

Built in 1970 and 1971, the Magnolia at Tyler center was the first major peripheral development for the Tyler Mall across the street. Over the years, the multi-store center housed a Zody's department store (above), Pic 'N Save–Big Lots, Alpha Beta grocery, Thrifty Drugs, and Goodyear Tires. More recently, the center has seen Home Base hardware and Computer City, both in the 1990s, as well as Staples, Pier 1, Sport Chalet, America's Tires, and Bed, Bath and Beyond. (Then image courtesy Daniel Balboa.)

A postcard view of Magnolia Avenue at Van Buren Boulevard around 1940 shows the still-standing 1910 Jenkins Building (right). For several years, the corners were home to competing drugstores, including Keystone Drug (above, center), which also had a location downtown. A new two-story building has since replaced the former Keystone, which was destroyed by fire. In 2008, a widened Van Buren eased traffic congestion at the intersection. (Then image courtesy JoAnne Pease-Simpson; now image courtesy Thomas D. Lamm.)

Seen below in 1962 is the 9514 Magnolia Avenue camera shop for Arlington Phototorium, a fixture near the intersection of Magnolia Avenue and Van Buren Boulevard since 1932. The shop relocated nearby to 3770 Van Buren Boulevard in 1965 and to 9590 Magnolia Avenue in 1982. Abraham's was owned by former city councilman and county supervisor Walt Abraham, while Davenport's Market has long since been home to an auto parts store. (Then image courtesy Velda and Norman Kelley.)

Designed by Seeley L. Pillar, the Greek Revival Arlington Library (below, around 1912) opened to the public in 1909. It was Riverside's first branch library. In 1927, the building received a major structural upgrade after being declared seismically unsafe. Until 1938, the rear of the building also housed the Arlington fire station. In June 2008, an 8,000-square-foot addition opened (above, left), nearly tripling the size of the library. (Then image courtesy JoAnne Pease-Simpson; now image courtesy Thomas D. Lamm.)

Public Library, Arlington, Cal.

Following the 1898 San Jacinto earthquake, Riverside County General Hospital moved to the corner of Magnolia Avenue and Harrison Street in Arlington. By the 1960s, the 1938 surgical wing (above, right) stood alongside a newly built addition (above, left). In 1998, after nearly 100 years in Riverside, the hospital relocated to Moreno Valley. Since 2001, the site has been the location for a shopping center anchored by a Lowe's home improvement store. (Then image courtesy Steve Lech; now image courtesy Thomas D. Lamm.)

As with many areas of Southern California during the immediate postwar years, large portions of central Riverside quickly transformed from farmland to suburban housing. Seen above in the mid-1950s is the Monticello Avenue storm drain as it slants northwest from the intersection of California Avenue and Monroe Street. By 1970, the land straddling California Avenue from Streeter Avenue to Van Buren Boulevard had been mostly developed, including the nearby California Square shopping center, which opened an Alpha Beta in 1957 and Dairy Queen in 1960.

Named after Maj. Gen. William G. Haan, Camp Haan (below, around 1941) was established in 1940 west of Highway 395–Interstate 215. The camp served several purposes during World War II, including antiaircraft training, debarkation point, and prisoner of war facility. After the war, most of the land was absorbed into adjacent March Air Force Base. In 1978, Riverside National Cemetery (above) opened on a large portion of the former camp. (Then image courtesy March Field Air Museum.)

From 1957 to 1989, Riverside International Raceway hosted all major racing circuits, including NASCAR, CART, IROC, IMSA, INDY, F1 and SCORE. Its proximity to Los Angeles led to numerous television programs and films, including Disney's *The Love Bug*. The site of the nine-turn, 3.3-mile track became Moreno Valley's master-planned Towngate development. Located near the former main grandstand (below) is Towngate Park, where a checkerboard motif offers subtle homage to the former racetrack. (Then image courtesy Riverside International Automotive Museum.)

CHAPTER 3

ABOVE TOWN

Above is a view of La Sierra looking northeast toward Mount San Gorgonio around 1968. In the immediate foreground is La Sierra College—now University—with the intersection of Pierce Street and Sierra Vista Avenue at far left. The large swath of farmland has since become part of the Riverwalk development. (Courtesy La Sierra University.)

Before Southern California's explosive postwar suburban development began, large swaths of Riverside consisted primarily of orange groves and related agricultural uses. Seen in the 1948 aerial above are Victoria Country Club (top), Victoria Hill (top left), and Victoria Avenue (left). The same view in 2005 shows the groves replaced with homes—built mostly between 1960 and 1980—and Polytechnic High School (lower left), which moved from present-day Riverside Community College to the corner of Victoria Avenue and Central Avenue in 1965. (Courtesy HistoricAerials.com.)

Even as late as 1948 (below), the Magnolia Center area of Riverside still contained large, undeveloped parcels. Within 10 years, the area was home to the Riverside Plaza and Brockton Arcade commercial centers. At lower left is Palm School with Magnolia Avenue diagonally slicing northward, crossing Brockton, Central, and Jurupa Avenues (top center). The area, seen above in 2005, is still dominated by the Riverside Plaza. At lower right is the Riverside Freeway as it crosses Central Avenue. (Courtesy HistoricAerials.com.)

Seen below in 1948 is the intersection of Magnolia Avenue at Tyler Street. Large-scale development would begin in earnest following the 1970 opening of Riverside's Tyler Mall (now Galleria at Tyler). Seen above in 2005 are several "big-box" commercial developments, including Target, Bed, Bath and Beyond, Staples, Office Depot, Toys R Us, Best Buy, and Circuit City. Once located just left of center was Magnolia Drive-In (now an ice rink). At lower left are Kaiser Hospital (1988) and Castle Park (1976). (Courtesy HistoricAerials.com.)

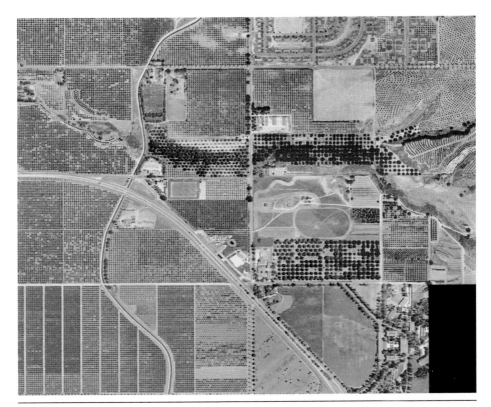

At lower right above is the Citrus Experiment Station, the forerunner to University of California Riverside, as seen in 1948. At top right is housing originally used by March Air Force Base. Note Highway 60 curving west toward downtown onto present-day University Avenue. Construction on the general campus began in the early 1950s. The oval track (above, center) is where University of California Riverside's student commons and iconic bell tower are now located. (Courtesy HistoricAerials.com.)

Seen above in 1967 is eastern Riverside where it meets the city of Moreno Valley, which incorporated in 1984. At top left is the Interstate 215–Highway 60 interchange. At right is Riverside International Raceway, which, after closing in 1989, made way for Moreno Valley's Towngate development. In 1992, the Moreno Valley Mall at Towngate (below, top right) opened, winning the mall war against a similar enclosed mall proposed for Riverside's Canyon Springs development (below, top left). (Courtesy HistoricAerials.com.)

BIBLIOGRAPHY

Hall, Joan H. *Cottages, Colonials and Community Places of Riverside, California*. Riverside, CA: Highgrove Press, 2003.

Klotz, Ester H. and Joan H. Hall. *Adobes, Bungalows, and Mansions of Riverside, California—Revisited*. Riverside, CA: Highgrove Press, 2004.

Lech, Steve. *Riverside: 1870–1940*. Charleston, SC: Arcadia Publishing, 2007.

————. *Riverside in Vintage Postcards*. Charleston, SC: Arcadia Publishing, 2005.

Lewis, Richard and Vincent Moses. *The Riverside Fire Department Presents—A Century of Service*. Riverside, CA: The Riverside Firemen's Benefit Association, 1983.

Patterson, Tom. *A Colony for California—Second Edition*. Riverside, CA: Riverside Museum Press, 1996.

————. *Landmarks of Riverside*. Riverside, CA: The Press-Enterprise Company, 1964.

Riverside Fire Department. *Souvenir of the City of Riverside—1906*. Riverside, CA: Riverside Museum Press, 1987 (historical reprint).

Sercl, Georgia Gordon. *Arlington*. Charleston, SC: Arcadia Publishing, 2007.

DISCOVER THOUSANDS OF LOCAL HISTORY BOOKS
FEATURING MILLIONS OF VINTAGE IMAGES

Arcadia Publishing, the leading local history publisher in the United States, is committed to making history accessible and meaningful through publishing books that celebrate and preserve the heritage of America's people and places.

Find more books like this at
www.arcadiapublishing.com

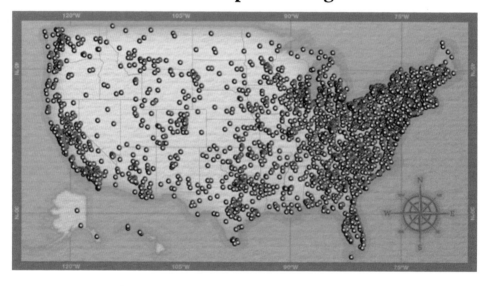

Search for your hometown history, your old stomping grounds, and even your favorite sports team.